Small Piglet Looks for Mommy

About Animal Babies

Published by Scholastic India Pvt. Ltd.
A subsidiary of Scholastic Inc., New York, 10012 (USA).
Publishers since 1920, with international operations in Canada, Australia, New Zealand, the United Kingdom, India, and Hong Kong.

For information regarding permission, write to:
Scholastic India Pvt. Ltd.
A-27, Ground Floor, Sigma Centre
Infocity-1, Sector 34, Gurgaon-122001 (India)

First edition: February 2016
This reprint edition: March 2026

ISBN-13: 978-81-7655-810-5

Printed in India at Shivam Offset Press, New Delhi

Small Piglet Looks for Mommy

About Animal Babies

Illustrations Vivekananda Roy Ghatak

SCHOLASTIC
New York Toronto London Auckland
Sydney New Delhi Hong Kong

The small piglet cannot find her mother.
She runs to the field and sees the cow
chewing the cud.
'Mommy?' she calls.

'This is not your Mommy,' says the calf. 'This is my Mommy.'
'Why don't you look near the pond?' asks the mother cow. 'You might find your Mommy there.'

The small piglet runs to the pond and
sees the duck swimming.
'Mommy?' she calls.

'This is not your Mommy,' say the ducklings. 'This is our Mommy.'
'Why don't you look near the big house?' asks the mother duck. 'You might find your Mommy there.'

The small piglet runs towards the big house and sees the dogs playing. 'Mommy?' she calls.

'This is not your Mommy,' say the pups. 'This is our Mommy.'

'Why don't you look in the stable?' asks the mother dog. 'You might find your Mommy there.'

The small piglet runs to the stable and sees the horses standing.
'Mommy?' she calls.
'This is not your Mommy,' says the foal. 'This is my Mommy.'
'Why don't you look near the chicken coop?' asks the mother mare. 'You might find your Mommy there.'

The small piglet runs to the chicken shed and sees the hen hatching her eggs.
'Mommy?' she calls.

'This is not your Mommy,' say the chicks. 'This is our Mommy.'

'Why don't you look near the hill?' asks the mother hen. 'You might find your Mommy there.'

The small piglet runs to the hill and sees the sheep grazing.
'Mommy?' she calls.

'This is not your Mommy,' says the lamb. 'This is my Mommy.'

'Why don't you look in the orchard?' asks the mother ewe. 'You might find your Mommy there.'

The small piglet runs to the orchard and
sees the goat eating leaves.
'Mommy?' she calls.
'This is not your Mommy,' says the kid.
'This is my Mommy.'

'Why don't you look in the old garage?' asks the mother goat. 'You might find your Mommy there.'

The small piglet runs to the old garage and sees the owl dozing.
'Mommy?' she calls.

‘This is not your Mommy,’ say the owlets.
‘This is our Mommy.’
‘Why don’t you look in the kitchen?’ asks the mother owl. ‘You might find your Mommy there.’

The small piglet runs to the kitchen and sees the cat drinking milk.
'Mommy?' she calls.
'This is not your Mommy,' say the kittens.
'This is our Mommy.'

'Why don't you look in the sty?' asks the mother cat. 'That is where your Mommy is.'

The small piglet runs to the sty and sees the pigs.
'Mommy!' she calls.
'There you are!' cries mother sow.
'Where have you been, Small Piglet?'

‘I was looking for you,’ answered the small piglet.
‘And I was looking for you,’ says the small piglet’s Mommy.

Baby Facts

ANIMALS	ANIMAL BABIES
Cow	Calf
Duck	Duckling
Horse	Foal
Hen	Chick
Sheep	Lamb
Goat	Kid
Owl	Owlet
Cat	Kitten
Pig	Piglet

About the Illustrator

Vivekananda Roy Ghatak graduated from the National Institute of Design, Ahmedabad, where he specialised in Animation Film Design. Primarily involved in animation for television, he is currently working as an animation director for a preschool TV show. He is also working on a short animation film of his own.